ME TOO

Copyright © 2024 by Teri Schure

All rights reserved. No part of this publication may be reproduced, in whole or in part, stored in a retrieval system, or transmitted in any form by any means—electronic, mechanical, photocopying, recording, or other—without written permission from the author.

For permission or other queries, write to:
Teri Schure, All Media, Inc., 124 Grove Avenue,
#401, Cedarhurst, NY 11516.

Cover & layout design:
www.kimmontefortebookdesign.com
Cover illustration: Teri Schure
Back cover photograph:
www.irynasosnovska.com

ISBN 978-1-7352214-4-1 (PB)
ISBN 978-1-7352214-5-8 (EB)

Library of Congress Control Number: 2024917504

Printed in the United States of America
10 9 8 7 6 5 4 3 2 1

ME TOO

A Poetic Timeline

TERI SCHURE

DEDICATION

I dedicate *Me Too: A Poetic Timeline* to my fourteen-year-old self, known back then as Theresa (Terry) Mahigel. Despite my objection, that same year, the spelling of my nickname was altered, and my last name was summarily and illegally changed.

Just like that, my persona suffered through a paralyzing heart-mind-and-body metamorphosis. I emerged wingless and in a perpetual state of fright, fight, and flight.

Without Terry Mahigel's grit, tenacity, and bravery, I would never have had the courage to publish this poetic chronology, which for decades was shrouded in shameful secrecy—
until now.

Yet, I am terrified of exposing and revealing my rawness, bareness, and vulnerability. And I pray my painful compilation won't cause my loved ones too much discomfort.

I held off sharing my lamentations until now because of their feelings—for fear of embarrassing or hurting my family. My family is everything to me, and I have no purpose or life without them.

But despite the fear, I know in my heart that I owe it to that young, naive, and hopeful girl to write it out. I've got no choice but to lay it all out there.

Because without her pain, her truth, and her written testimony, there is no me.

TO THE READER

Me Too: A Poetic Timeline is about surviving abuse and navigating through its lifelong, interminable aftereffects.

It's an emotional roller coaster of a read, and I hope you won't judge me negatively.

But I know some of you will.

And that's okay.

Because I also know that I'm not alone.

There are a lot of us out there.

Too many of us.

That's why I decided to share my trauma.

For them. For us. The survivors.

For all the "liars," "sluts," "troublemakers," "black sheep," and the ones with big mouths who talk too much.

And for those who are afraid to talk at all …

I see you.

And I'm with you.

Because I am you.

THE TIMELINE

The Teller．．．．．．．．．．．．．．．．．．．．．．．．．xiii	Seven Words．．．．．．．．．．．．．．．．．．．．．35
Theresa．．．．．．．．．．．．．．．．．．．．．．．．．．．．．1	The Legend of Us．．．．．．．．．．．．．．．．．36-37
Footsteps．．．．．．．．．．．．．．．．．．．．．．．．．．．2	Pants on Fire．．．．．．．．．．．．．．．．．．．．．38
Those Things．．．．．．．．．．．．．．．．．．．．．．．．3	Unfinished Business．．．．．．．．．．．．．．．．．39
My Nonet．．．．．．．．．．．．．．．．．．．．．．．．．．．4	What Was I Thinking?．．．．．．．．．．．．．．．．40
Who?．．．．．．．．．．．．．．．．．．．．．．．．．．．．．．．5	Recall．．．．．．．．．．．．．．．．．．．．．．．．．．．．．．41
You．．．．．．．．．．．．．．．．．．．．．．．．．．．．．．．．．6	One Phone Call Away．．．．．．．．．．．．．．．42-43
My Delta Wings．．．．．．．．．．．．．．．．．．．．．．7	Triggers．．．．．．．．．．．．．．．．．．．．．．．．．．．．44
Goodbye．．．．．．．．．．．．．．．．．．．．．．．．．．．．8	Eye Contact．．．．．．．．．．．．．．．．．．．．．．．．．45
The Last Time．．．．．．．．．．．．．．．．．．．．．．．．9	But．．．．．．．．．．．．．．．．．．．．．．．．．．．．．．．．．．46
A House with Very Bad Bones．．．．．．．．．．10	Are You Reading This?．．．．．．．．．．．．．．．．47
Fly．．．．．．．．．．．．．．．．．．．．．．．．．．．．．．．．．．11	Bricks．．．．．．．．．．．．．．．．．．．．．．．．．．．．48-49
I Am a Giant．．．．．．．．．．．．．．．．．．．．．．．．．12	Beep, Beep．．．．．．．．．．．．．．．．．．．．．．．．．．50
A Vision Foretold．．．．．．．．．．．．．．．．．．．．．13	I Hear a Symphony．．．．．．．．．．．．．．．．．．．51
Peace by Piece．．．．．．．．．．．．．．．．．．．．．．．14	Trading Places．．．．．．．．．．．．．．．．．．．．．52-53
The Aftermath．．．．．．．．．．．．．．．．．．．．．．．15	Alpha Men．．．．．．．．．．．．．．．．．．．．．．．．．．54
Blind．．．．．．．．．．．．．．．．．．．．．．．．．．．．．．．．16	Obstacles．．．．．．．．．．．．．．．．．．．．．．．．．．．．55
Last Confession．．．．．．．．．．．．．．．．．．．．．．17	The Rose．．．．．．．．．．．．．．．．．．．．．．．．．．56-57
Is It You?．．．．．．．．．．．．．．．．．．．．．．．．．．．．18	#MeToo．．．．．．．．．．．．．．．．．．．．．．．．．．．．．．58
Deny, Deny, Deny．．．．．．．．．．．．．．．．．．．．．19	Let It Go．．．．．．．．．．．．．．．．．．．．．．．．．．．．．59
Teh-Teh?．．．．．．．．．．．．．．．．．．．．．．．．．．．．20	No Joy．．．．．．．．．．．．．．．．．．．．．．．．．．．．．．．60
Bruised．．．．．．．．．．．．．．．．．．．．．．．．．．．．．．21	Where I Come from Is Who I Am．．．．61
Memories．．．．．．．．．．．．．．．．．．．．．．．．．．．22	Cloud Cover．．．．．．．．．．．．．．．．．．．．．．．．．62
Endings．．．．．．．．．．．．．．．．．．．．．．．．．．．．．23	No Laughing Matter, But．．．．．．．．．．．．．．63
Seven Years．．．．．．．．．．．．．．．．．．．．．．．．．．24	The Hourglass．．．．．．．．．．．．．．．．．．．．．．．．64
The Secret．．．．．．．．．．．．．．．．．．．．．．．．．．．25	The Words I Never Said．．．．．．．．．．．．．．．65
Fancy Pants．．．．．．．．．．．．．．．．．．．．．．．．．．26	The Unraveling．．．．．．．．．．．．．．．．．．．．．．．66
Lullaby and Goodnight．．．．．．．．．．．．．．．．27	A Work in Progress．．．．．．．．．．．．．．．．．．．．67
She Already Knew．．．．．．．．．．．．．．．．．．．．28	I See You．．．．．．．．．．．．．．．．．．．．．．．．．．．．．68
Write It Out．．．．．．．．．．．．．．．．．．．．．．．．．．29	One Holiday at a Time．．．．．．．．．．．．．．．．69
Make a Wish．．．．．．．．．．．．．．．．．．．．．．．．．30	Lifeline．．．．．．．．．．．．．．．．．．．．．．．．．．．．．．．70
Name Game．．．．．．．．．．．．．．．．．．．．．．．．．．31	The End．．．．．．．．．．．．．．．．．．．．．．．．．．．．．．71
Bully Boy．．．．．．．．．．．．．．．．．．．．．．．．．．．．32	Somewhere Under the Rainbow．．．72-73
The System．．．．．．．．．．．．．．．．．．．．．．．．．．33	The End End．．．．．．．．．．．．．．．．．．．．．．．．．．74
The Things I Know．．．．．．．．．．．．．．．．．．．34	

ME TOO: A POETIC TIMELINE

The Teller

She's a brooder, but she can be sardonically funny.

She's a storyteller, but spreadsheets were her bread and butter.

She's been through hell and back, but she's not bitter.

She started out poor in an all-female world, living with
Grandma, Great-grandma, and her teenage mother.

A dead man's collection of classical books changed her trajectory.
But even before the books, her hard-wired brain was
chock-full of words writing themselves.

The twenty-six letters in the alphabet served her purpose well.
She took those letters and created reams of writings and
untold thousands of diary and journal entries.

And she was adeptly genius at writing in code.

Her Me Too poems go as far back as 1967
before the MeToo movement was even a thing.

Although she knows all too well that Me Too was always a thing.

This is her story. This is her tome.

1967–2024

Theresa

Theresa. What a beautiful name.
That's what you said when we first met
in my chaotic, poor-girl era.

You promised you would
provide me with a stable life.
You promised a lot of things.

Now, I'm not Theresa
with a beautiful name,
but someone to ridicule,
bully, and harass.

Now I'm Theresa the Greaser,
the Mod Martian, the one who
quickly blossomed before your eyes.

You told me I was safe and sound,
but oh, no, I wasn't.

You yanked me out of the simmering embers
and threw me into a raging fire.

9/28/1967

Footsteps

I'm reading by the dim glow of
the hurricane table lamp.

But my body is shuddering, and
my trembling hands make
reading impossible.

So I turn to writing and pen
the words in quivery code.

First reading, then writing,
all the while waiting ...

... for the footsteps ...

... for the shadow of two feet at the
bottom of the bedroom door ...

Shhh ...

10/16/1968

Those Things

There are those things
that sit silently.

Mum's the word.

Those things
undercover.

Those unspeakable,
soul-crushing
things.

12/25/1969

My Nonet

The piano was my treasured gift.
An opulent bedroom presence
the last remains of my past,
my instrument of choice.
I played it daily
until the fire.
Then it was
my door
lock.

5/19/1970

Who?

I thought if I called you something familial,
you would wake up and leave me alone.

It was the first time I ever called anyone that.

You guffawed at the familial noun I used.

"Who?"

I never called you that again.

And you never woke up.

12/31/1971

You

The crimson ball has slowly sunk from view,
the piano blocks the door in the hope you can't get in.

I sit in darkness, in fear of you,
and paint my soul in strokes of hate and sin.

The tranquil beach is empty, but for one;
I gaze into the sun until I'm blind.

In my head, I see the night and plan to run,
but nowhere is safe; death visions fill my mind.

I'm in a rage; my fears all bear your name.
Concupiscence has consumed my brightest light.

My mind replays my guilt and filth and shame,
I'm drowning, and I've lost the will to fight.

Tonight, I'll sit and wait before a canvas dark in hue,
and paint deformed, abhorrent stains of you.

12/12/1972

My Delta Wings

The sunset was before me,
the airport runway to the left.

The wind blew through my tightly coiffed
bun as I drove with the top down in my
electric blue Karmann Ghia.

I adored the car, but I hated that it was
his absolution payoff.

A recompense ensuring that
I would keep my mouth shut.

At twenty, it was the happiest day of my life.

Free from all that weighed me down.

Emancipated.   Liberated.   Extricated.

Free from him at long last.

12/24/1973

Goodbye

Whoever you are, whoever you might have been, understand
that I am left with one choice, one choice only, that's it.

And now the worry of where and how and the fear of that dreary,
illegal place is combined with the knowledge that I'm unfit.

Someday, you'll see; someday, I'll break free in the hope
that you'll come back as mine.

Sadly, not now, not like this, but I will see you, oh yes,
in a better place and time.

Please forgive me, little one; I have no choice but to say goodbye
and help you go away.

I'm alone, I'm weary, and in desperate need of a miracle like you,
but not today.

And, oh my, the glory when I see you in my colorful dreams.
Sometimes, you're a feisty he, and other times, a mischievous she.

But when I awake, I know in my heart that the feisty and the mischievous
will have to wait. Because anywhere is surely safer than with me.

I'm not safe; I'm not safe inside like you. I'm trapped with a
hungry lion, desperately trying to escape his gnarly den.

That's why I need your fragile self to forgive me so I can
feel relief that you'll come back to visit me again.

I need you to understand that I'm currently fixated only on my survival.
But next time, I promise to wrap you up in my loving arms
upon your miraculous arrival.

Until such time, tiny one, whoever you are, whoever you might have been,
I pray you will return to me.

And I promise when it's my time for someone to finally arrive,
it will be your precious face that I will see.

4/12/1974

The Last Time

I reluctantly attended your
mother's funeral.

And you were your usual asshole,
touchy-feely-grabby self.

As you locked the door, I was
locked in frozen fear, unable
to make a move.

In the corner of your dead
mother's bedroom, you were
aggressive and confident,

with the blackest of eyes, even
though they were usually a
beautiful sky blue.

But this time, I threatened you,
but good.

And this time, unlike all
the other times,

I scared the hell out of you instead
of the other way around.

And just so you know, I'm not
done with you yet.

5/5/1975

A House with Very Bad Bones

Our low-income housing apartment was humble and lacking, but it was my home, my safe place.

The other house—hidden on a dead end in a toney town—was a palace, but it was never my home.

It was a hazardous edifice disguised as a home—a house with very bad bones.

An unsafe dwelling with scores of code violations that he created, and she ignored.

Until she, too, became a violator and
I became the condemned.

7/4/1976

Fly

I told you secrets that I don't often share. Your tenderness made me feel safe, which is why I laid myself so bare.

You're incredibly kind and gentle, and you've touched me with the sincerity of your heart. Most importantly, you assured me that I could trust you from the very start.

When I'm with you, I'm not afraid of what might be lurking in the night. Our hours spent together have taught me to reject the dark and honor the light.

So, it's because you saved me from myself that I feel so bad that what I am about to do will surely make you incredibly sad.

I tried to love you because you so wholeheartedly and unconditionally loved me. You saw me as a soaring seagull with a daisy flying over a rainbow in your poetry.

And I lament the stormy tide that washed away the seagull, the daisy, and the colorful sky. I wanted to quell the surging swells and soar so high I could touch heaven; I really did try.

I'm not your soaring seagull; I never was. My wings are irretrievably broken, which is why I must so regrettably say goodbye.

But I will never forget how you rooted for me to spiral, not downward, but upward against the roiling seas and fly.

6/6/1977

I Am a Giant

It took a lifetime to realize
that I am a giant when compared
to your tiny, ruthless self.

People like you hide
their insecurities
by bullying and
abusing people like me.

You're not powerful enough
to extinguish my light.

You don't know it yet,
but the evil you have sown
is your curse.

Your sickness will undo you.

No one heals himself
by wounding another.

You have no power over me.

The power is mine, all mine.

8/1/1978

A Vision Foretold

I knew you were running out of time,
and you knew it, too.
You always knew best.
You always knew everything.
The one who couldn't read or write.
Your last words were well thought out.
A vision you foretold.
"Stay away from him."
"He's no good for you."
"Walk away."
Words of wisdom before
they took your lung.
Should have,
could have,
would have.
But I didn't.

9/6/1979

Peace by Piece

I want to be whole.
I want to break away
from the finger-pointing,
the grudge-holding,
and my unfixable
broken self.

But it's impossible
to find peace
with the knowledge
that an apology
or a mere admission
of wrongdoing is
improbable.

8/13/1980

The Aftermath

It's not a quick demise like
a fatal accident
or stage four cancer.

It's a slow burn,
with no before,
just after.

A life sentence in
a prison with
invisible bars.

9/24/1981

Blind

Have you ever come upon a
photo of yourself with someone
who you thought was your person,
but now they're not, and you feel
so stupid, and you can't stop asking
yourself, "How didn't I see it?"

6/20/1982

Last Confession

When I saw you last, you were
at death's door.
You confessed that you knew.
Your last confession was like a
knife to my heart.
I told you that I think of him
only once in a great while,
but that was a lie
to appease your last guilty day on earth.
You told me that was your cross to bear.
Yours?
Only when you were
gone and cold
did I confess to you that I lied.
I think of him every minute, no,
every second of every day.
I screamed it so loud the nurse ran in.
My cross to bear.
Not because of him, but because
you knew and didn't save me.

3/22/1983

Is It You?

I tied myself into a knot today.
Not because I wanted to but
because I made a promise
to someone almost nine years
ago to the day. Is it you?
Did you come back to me?

4/29/1983

Deny, Deny, Deny

Every time I see
a pair of cowboy boots
I want to kick you
in the stomach,

like you kicked me.

I want to smirk at you
curled up in a fetal ball.

And then deny, deny, deny

as you convulse
and writhe in pain.

1/15/1984

Teh-Teh?

When the piano
morphed into a crib,
it became my safety net.

I was late-night sneaking,
but that angelic face was peeking.
My savior, my tiny musette.

Teh? Teh-Teh?
She called out behind the
wooden slats in glee.
Now, I can only imagine the
names she calls me.

But no matter how she feels
or what she might think,
she's still lodged deep
within my disordered heart.

And there she will remain
until the day that I depart.

5/22/1985

Bruised

I can take the
black and blues.

It's the broken heart that
you've forever bruised.

I'll be free of you,
you'll see.

But you'll never
be free of me.

1/20/1986

Memories

Funny how
the memory works.

There are those tender things
I fight to remember.

And then there are those
nightmarish things
I fight to forget.

The frightful
memories fester
and seep deep down.

Deep down
into my soul.

I know the pain
will never abate.

Not even when I let
the memories out.

So, I make space for them
deep within me.

11/26/1987

Endings

Two broken people
could equal
a disastrous ending.

Especially when one
wields the hammer
and the other is
cracked wide open
and bleeding out.

Endings might just
be more beautiful
than beginnings.

2/29/1988

Seven Years

Seven
wretched
years.

That's what
I told you.

Seven years
you replied,

it could have
been worse.

You were wrong,
so wrong.

Seven years
was a lifetime,
leaving the rest
of them
in shambles.

4/3/1989

The Secret

Being unable
to share
my secret
was a heavy
burden.

I was so busy
protecting
the secret
I was unable
to protect
myself.

4/3/1990

Fancy Pants

"Be careful," she warned all uppity
as she handed me my drink.

"This Waterford wine glass cost
me two hundred dollars."

Later that evening,
when I broke it,

I cursed myself for
not demanding plastic.

12/24/1991

Lullaby and Goodnight

To lie in my child's bed when she is gone
is as calming as anything I know.

To fall asleep, with her books scattered around me,
is to admit that I have never been so tired
and so lonely for the warmth of her tiny body.

I feel hopeless and try to find more than
my two reasons for living.

I'm alone, not knowing what I should
or shouldn't reveal.

I know that my cramped escapes and
stumbling blocks need to be faced,
and I need to accept my world.

I'm at peace in her bed because there still
remain these places, occupied by my
beloved children, and all I need is just one
who understands and finds me here.

For I know that she will lie down beside me
and embrace my broken body.

1/1/1992

She Already Knew

It was my turn to testify, and it was a disclosure I was terrified to reveal.

We were in a good place—so emotionally good that I warned her not to come to court that day.

I wanted to tell her—I really did—but I was afraid I'd lose her.

And anyway, she was always trying to stop me from telling.

Because she already knew.

She wanted me to shut up and take it.

Just like she did.

As the opposing lawyer prodded and the judge warned, I had no choice but to tell.

The shameful words felt sleazy and slimy, and painful.

Oh, so frightfully painful.

But I never wanted her to feel the pain of it, which is why I said it behind her back.

11/14/1993

Write It Out

Am I
a poet
chasing rhymes
or
a writer
seeking words?

No matter,
poet
or
writer
or
rhymes
or
words,

I need to
spell it.

I need to
spill it.

It all needs
to come out.

One way
or another,

I need to make
myself whole.

9/24/1994

Make a Wish

Make a wish, they tell me,
as the plethora of candles
burn bright.

As I try to blow them all out,
I wish for you what you
wish for me.

It's my way of wishing that karma
comes for you hard without wishing
injurious things.

I know how you feel about me.

If you're wondering, I feel the same
way about you,

but 2.0 ...

... Make that 4.0

4/3/1995

Name Game

I want to write his name.

I want to say his name.

So everyone will know.

But I'm a spineless coward.

When will it ever end?

Perhaps I will write it at his death.

Or perhaps never.

12/25/1996

Bully Boy

My sense of self-worth is larger than your tiny mind.
You hide behind your psychosis; I know your kind.

You're not powerful enough to extinguish my light.
Your quagmire of ugliness is the reason I fight.

And eventually, your sickness will undo you, you'll see.
You will never be able to heal yourself by wounding me.

11/25/1997

The System

How many times
do sexual perverts
and molesters
get to walk away
scot-free

while their victims
are shunned
and accused
of being liars
or worse?

How is it possible to
move on from so many
blind eyes?

How does one find
closure without
resolution?

When will the system
crush the men and boys
who destroy and crush
the lives of so many
innocent women
and girls?

It's pure evil.
It's pure sickness.

And the system
is nowhere to be found.

9/16/1998

The Things I Know

When the calamity cracked me open,
it forced me to remove myself.

I slammed shut my glazed eyes
and suffered through it.

The jack-hammering drove me
to think of the essential things, like living.

Surviving brought with it clarity and
empathy for the suffering of so many others.

But sometimes the calamity, the suffering,
and surviving left me with no benefit at all.

Only resentment for those who told me to count
my blessings or that time heals all wounds,
when I know my wounds are fatal.

The things I know forced me to be
gangster tough, to survive another day.

But I also know that as tough as I am,
I will never be tough enough to forget.

8/12/1999

Seven Words

She phoned and accused me of stirring up trouble.
"Why don't you ask him yourself?"
"I think I will," she answered confidently before she hung up.
I anxiously waited and waited and waited.
Then the phone rang, and it was her.
"Did you ask him?"
Silence on the other end.
"Did you ask him?
More silence, and then, "Yes."
"What did he say?"
Silence.
"Hello? What did he say?"
The silence was killing me, although I was already half dead.
Then she took a deep breath in before speaking.
I held my own breath, waiting.
"Please, tell me what he said, in his exact words."
His seven words chilled me to the bone.
"That's the way I was back then."

11/20/2000

The Legend of Us

You and I have a history.

Are we a legend, or did we merely live out a predetermined sequence of events that resulted in the sad story of us?

We've both had our fair share of slip-ups and poor decisions. Perhaps we'll reunite somewhere out there, somewhere other than this bittersweet earth. But probably not.

When we danced in that crummy kitchen, it was transcendent. Yes, transcendent because you chose me, and you pulled me in close—so close that I was able to breathe in all of you.

If I had known our best moments and random triumphs were fleeting, I would have cherished them more than I did. There were moments I wished we could relive, moments I wanted to last forever.

And then there were others I've spent a lifetime wishing away. I couldn't keep quiet because the telling kept me sane. And yet, the truth did not set me free. Instead, it set in motion a roller coaster of cruel denials.

Set in motion by not one, not two, but three of you. I cared not for two and three—just you. You were always the one. I'm sorry I couldn't change the moments that destroyed us. As you know, those moments were in someone else's groping hands.

Teri Schure

We crisscrossed in and out of each other's lives a few times. In all but one of those times, something always told me we would see each other again. But not this time.

In the beginning, you chose me to dance, but in the end, you threw me away. What I don't know and never asked is if you wanted me. Over the years, I imagined that you did not.

I wonder now if you regret the day I was born, and I wouldn't blame you if you did because we both got tangled up in all of it. And you know the manhandling truth because it happened to you, too.

We were more alike than you or I cared to admit. So many times, out of anger, you did not choose your words wisely.

If it wasn't for you ...

You probably didn't know, but those five words stung. The stinging was real and as painful as getting a tattoo, although I never got one. Or maybe I did.

A tattoo of us, etched forever on my broken heart.

3/1/2001

Pants on Fire

It took a deadly attack for you, the proxy, to phone. Then you called me a liar.
I know way more than you think, and your lying pants are the ones on fire.

Let's both take a lie detector test before you gaslight and so unkindly crucify.
We both know that will never happen because, unlike you, lie detectors don't lie.

You told your BFF I was a thorn in the side and the family's black sheep.
Her cruelty and diarrhea of the mouth left me gutted and in a shattered heap.

She blabbed that I was cut out of their will. Her crushing monologue had no end.
This hateful rhetoric is what I needed to hear from your moronic, drunken friend?

I'm seeping in black, but I'm no sheep, just our family's sacrificial lamb.
You finally did it; you pushed me out. I see right through your jealous sham.

You're the one with all the secrets, and we both know why.
Liar, liar pants on fire. Your shrewdest move was to turn a blind eye.

9/11/2001

Unfinished Business

We are an unresolved distraction of monumental proportions.
Our closure is as elusive as the opening and reopening of our festering wounds.

The wounds cut deep but not as deep as your betrayal.
I may have been a lot of things,
but disloyal was never one of them.

We are an open-ended bundle of pain with no closure in sight.

One of us needs to finish up already.
Since you're the oldest, I'm expecting it
to be you.

8/15/2002

What Was I Thinking?

Why did I make
so many ruinous
choices in my life?

I think it's because
I was convinced that
I was damaged goods,

and undeserving of
anything better.

9/11/2003

Recall

Decades have passed,
but in the dead of night,
I still go over it and over it,
again and again and again.
The recall is relentless.
The recall is slowly killing me.

When I finally spoke out
and said something to the
one person who could heal me,
I heart-wrenchingly lost her.

Regrets? Not really.

Because the countless times
I shut my mouth
and said nothing at all to the
one person who could heal me,
I heart-wrenchingly lost myself.

10/15/2004

One Phone Call Away

When we met at fourteen, we were an unlikely team;
me from the hood, you from a place more like Hollywood.

We were playful and nonsensical while also dealing with warlike strife.
Was it a mere coincidence that we both had a dysfunctional family life?

I was a bundle of nerves each and every day, but you, courageous you,
promised me that you were always one phone call away.

When we couldn't see each other face-to-face,
my pink princess phone cord was so short and so tangled
I felt handicapped and stuck in one place.

Like my life, I was stuck, stuck in emotional quicksand,
desperately trying not to allow the muddy slurry to hold sway.
But thank God, you were always one phone call away.

We sported pigtails, snuck out of the house,
and sometimes swam in strangers' pools.
Years later, you settled into a fairy-tale life while
I jetted around with a legion of fools.

I joined a circus for a few heartbreaking years.
Your life was idyllic until it was your turn
to shed a thousand tears.

I fell off a cliff, down, down, down,
in a terrifying free fall.
And, unfortunately for me,
I had no one to call.

When we met a lifetime later, both of us
were in knocked-sideways disarray.
But then you so sweetly reminded me that
you were back, and only one phone call away.

9/16/2005

Triggers

It doesn't take all that much.
A smell, a photo, or an unwanted touch
to set my brain on fire
and activate the mental trip wire,
stretched tight and low,
willing the hot wire not to blow.
I check obituaries for the news
that will go a long way to diffuse
the mind triggers of the past
and give me back my life at long last.

7/15/2006

Eye Contact

Take that
which haunts you
and embrace it.

Don't be afraid,
to face it.

You have to
look it in the eye.

Because it's not going
anywhere, no matter
how hard you try.

10/18/2007

But

I love you, but
if it wasn't for you,
there is so much more
I could and would have done.

I love you, but
you're going out like that?
No makeup, eye shadow,
or lipstick, with your hair so frizzy?

I love you, but
why can't you be more like her?
She's athletic, confident, and obeys
all my rules.

I love you, but
what you said was hurtful to me,
and I've now heard it from the
East Coast to the West Coast.

I love you, but
you were twenty-one, and
when I asked him, he said
that's the way he was back then.

I love you, but
I have a family to worry about,
and you're ruining everything
for me.

I love you, but
goodbye.

2/26/2008

Are You Reading This?

If you're reading this, I know you
still care for me.

Hate is synonymous with love,
so thank you for being out there,
somewhere, looking me up.

I look you up, too.

If you're reading this, I need you to
know that I'm afraid we've missed
our chance at one last try.

One last try before we die.

If you're reading this, I need you to
know that I'm here, waiting for you.

And for those of you who just
happen to be reading this:

Seize the moment and reach out
to your long-lost you-know-who.

5/9/2009

Bricks

One brick, two bricks, three bricks,
coming at me from left and right.
Brick after painful brick,
with seemingly no end in sight.

Some bricks broke my spirit,
while others broke my trust.
I was knocked down but not out
and obsessed with crushing their
brick-slinging bloodlust.

When I picked myself up and brushed myself off,
my first thought was to throw the bricks back.
But then I asked myself, why should I be sullied
by an undignified counterattack?

And then a lightbulb went off. I'll use words!
Paste and bind them to protect and insulate.
I'll mortar myself using the characters of the alphabet,
to quell the character-assassinating, brick-baiting hate.

Let me hit them back with words instead of bricks,
by utilizing A-B-C-D-E-F-G.
I'll disarm them with vowels and consonants,
with the help of H-I-J-K-L-M-N-O-P.

I'll build a mighty fortress with mortared words,
cementing them between Q-R-S-T.
I'll shake the haters up by spilling through spelling,
U-V-W-X-Y-Z.

So, I used the alphabet to word-fortify against their attacks.
And I'll admit, those bricks initially brought me to my knees.
But now I'm safe and sound, all bricked up within and without.
My safehold, all in ABCs.

3/4/2010

Beep, Beep

She drives aimlessly, the rain pounding her windshield, until she realizes she is far from home, with a phone and a wallet but no bra.

She sees a rubber roadrunner in the crest of a wave. It's drowning, and she knows how that feels.

Behind her is a dune of sand fighting against the rising tide crashing up against it. She's teary and weary as she reaches out for beep, beep. Maybe if she saves him, she can save herself.

The roiling sea terrifies her, but she wants that rubber toy, come hell or high water. Since she's already in hell, she wades out into the deep for beep, beep—it's his fault she slips in and under.

A frigid wave crushes her, and she is shoved face down onto the sandy ocean floor. She's petrified but eerily resigned until she's catapulted to the surface.

Then she claws for the shore and hears a loud and frightened voice asking if she's okay.

She shouts yes, but she knows that she is doomed.

8/18/2011

I Hear a Symphony

The wind rustles through the
cypress trees, while the sparrows
perch like Christmas ornaments
and harmonize in the waning light.
It's chilly, but I sit and shiver,
grateful for the symphony,
the resin lion in plain sight.
I feel so much, yet it's never enough.
I wonder what they're doing
and wait.

10/14/2012

Trading Places

If you try to be me, I'll try to be you.
Then, for each other, we'll know what to do.

If you look at me through my eyes,
there will be no need to wear my protective disguise.

Because you'll be able to see that my inner child is in fear,
and the reason for my insecurities will be crystal clear.

You'll see that I'm not nearly as strong as I appear.
You'll see that I feel more and more pain with each passing year.

Then, it will be your turn to take off your mask.
And you'll have no choice but to tell me your true feelings when I ask.

I'll see that when you want to cry, you scream.
I'll see that you, like me, are not as tough as you seem.

I'll see that you are going over the brink.
I'll see that you love me much more than I think.

When you look at me reflected in your view,
the picture is distorted by my ego—and yours, too.

Look at me without the deep complexes of our past.
Open your heart and relate to me at last.

Let's open our minds—I'll become you, and you'll become me.
And I'm sure we'll be shocked and saddened by what we both see.

I'll see that you need understanding and to belong.
You'll see that I understood what you needed all along.

I'll see that you are weary of the games we play.
You'll see that I pray for you to love me every single day.

If I see your suffering and your unrelenting pain,
I will never again be so quick to place blame.

If you see the reasons why I cry and complain,
you'll see that the two of us are very much the same.

If I am you and you are me,
we can finally end this torture and agree,
to work on improving the relationship
and make it the very best that it can be.

And maybe we can finally live together
in peace and harmony.

So, let's trade places.

Let's open our eyes and see
what happens to the two of us

when I become you,
and you become me.

4/3/2013

Alpha Men

"This is a man's job," he spewed with arrogant confidence.

"This business is dominated by us," he boasted.

"What can you bring to the table?" he asked.

Answer him wisely. The power is in his hands. A man's table? A man's world?

Alpha men—born from women.

Amid hurdles and miracles, the egg lies in wait.

Out of millions, one male cell finds its way in.

The weakling girl transforms. Now she's the protector—the one in charge.

She discovers the beginning is the hardest. The most challenging. The riskiest.

She's unnerved but undaunted. She monitors and delights in quickening, an awakening, a flutter, and then a forceful kick.

Inner strength and power reveal themselves from deep within.

Patiently waiting for months and months while nourishing and supporting, discovering that life is resilient and sacrifice is quiet, she finds the courage to labor, push, and deliver.

She is bolstered by the belief that survival is key—reassured that anything is possible.

When the miracle arrives, she makes a promise to crack and shatter.

First, the table, then the world.

3/8/2014

Obstacles

I have tried
not to greet
the obstacles
with victimhood
and self-pity.
I have instead
welcomed
the obstacles
as opportunities
to grow
in resilience
and strength.

10/3/2015

The Rose

The rose fell out today as I rearranged my journals.
I gently picked it up and pressed it against my nose,
praying for the faintest hint of scent.

But the redolence of the flower was long gone, like him.
Then I placed it close to my heart and thought back twenty-one years.

It was a grueling day at work.
Flowers for valentines were delivered all day, but not for me.

"Snap out of it, kid," was my mantra.

On the train ride home, the fragrance of the hundreds of bouquets masked
the cigarette smell from the only car that had seats.

At my front door, I saw twelve of the deepest red roses I had ever seen.

The card brought me to my knees.
I never knew my eleven-year-old grump had those words in him.

I sat on the cold concrete, basked in euphoria
until he flew into my arms, preening.
Then I hugged and kissed him all over his perfect little face
as he giggled and squirmed.

TERI SCHURE

The flowers left him broke, he explained proudly.
The florist gave him a discount.

He pointed out that the vase was lavender—my favorite color,
even though the flower lady told him purple and red didn't go together.

I thought they went together perfectly imperfectly like us,
although I never told him that.

I never told him half of what I should have, and now it's too late.

I set the rose so hyper-carefully between the two blank pages it fell from.

If you ever come upon this dried-out flower, treat it gently.
Be oh-so-careful with it.

For it is a treasure,
and very fragile.

2/14/2016

#MeToo

In a surprising turn of events,
my prayers were answered with
five letters shoved into one hashtag word.

At fourteen, I tried to tell a few people,
but their silence was heartbreakingly absurd.

Years later, I told anyone who would listen,
but I was already hopelessly inured.

I was both the victim and the villain,
so in order to heal, I needed to be heard.

He who destroyed me became their king,
while I became their gallows bird.

10/15/2017

Let It Go

There are over 460,000 of us out there. Every year, 460,000 are defiled in the land of the free, the home of the brave.

The bad guys move on, telling no one of their bad behavior. All is forgotten.

But not us. We can never forget. The wounds fester and spread.

We never heal.

And when we tell, we're shunned, called sluts, liars, disowned.

The bad guys get to live their lives while we live with depression, drug abuse, alcoholism, and the effects of PTSD.

And why, please tell me why, is the burden of proof on us?

Why do they get to live a beautiful life while we serve a life sentence?

Let it go. Release it.

Let it go and release it to where?

How does someone let go of the most devastating thing that ever happened to them?

How does a young girl release the nightmarish memories that come back to her in flashbacks, night terrors, paralyzing phobias, and myriad addictions?

Our lives are ruined, so please stop making it worse by telling us to let it go.

And just so you know, we really want to let the whole damn thing go.

Nobody would ever want to live like this.

11/23/2017

No Joy

Joy to the world, but no joy here.
No joy, no joy, only sadness and fear.

I try to remember the things that used to mean so much.
My grandmother's smile, my mother's touch.

But year after year, I can't seem to let go
of the saddest moments I will ever know.

I wish the pain would go away,
so I can enjoy just one lousy, joyful day.

I want to feel alive and whole
and not allow those moments to take such a tragic toll.

I somehow need to figure out a way
to find the light and keep the darkness at bay.

But try as I might, I find no joy, no joy during this or any season.

He stole my joy; he stole my everything.

He is the reason.

12/25/2018

Where I Come from Is Who I Am

The fond and not-so-fond memories are my bedrock, like it or not.
The family, the friends, the breakups, the makeups, and all the wondrous things
tucked in between—tell the story of me.
My humble beginnings have stayed with me long after everything else
has begun to wither and fade.
From time to time, my first this and my first that
come back to me in hazy, dazing flashbacks.
Some are beautiful; some are discomposing.
My first snowstorm, my first home, my first love, my first fear,
a kiss, a sunset, a flash of lightning followed by earth-shattering thunder,
the aroma of freshly mowed grass I mowed myself.
A heartbreak or two, or three, or four,
or maybe more.
Despite the pain, the sorrows, and the demons, I miss both the joy and the ache.
If only I could go back and feel everything all over again.
Feel everything for the first time—the good and the bad.
Well, not the really bad.
The worst of the worst, I would courageously stomp out.
I would crush him like those cockroaches that covered our tenement kitchen walls.
But I would go back for the rest of it.
A longer hug, a deeper love, especially for myself,
back when my precious life was ahead of me and my journey was still determinable.
If only I could turn back the clock to where I come from just once
before the end of my time.

4/3/2019

Cloud Cover

Just like that, life closes in like
a hulk of fast-moving storm clouds.

They're so dark and so dense,
they block everything else out.

I try to push them away,
but they're immovable.

And from experience,
I know they're not moving any time soon.

I'll assess the storm damage
once it moves through me.

But until then,
I'll put on my happy face.

9/7/2020

No Laughing Matter, But …

There is nothing funny about the MeToo movement, although
I feel compelled to share this one-time-only event.

I've been shoving the inconceivable down, down, down for so many
years that nowadays, don't ask if you don't want me to tell.

I've been sitting so gaggingly silent for so long that

I'll Me-Too you, even if you don't ask.

Over dinner one night, a guy friend curiously queried, "What did he do?"
I proceeded to spell it out but spared him the gory details.

He stared at me quietly as I finished my MeToo monologue.
I figured he felt my pain.

"Oh, okay," he finally said awkwardly,
"but I meant, what did he do for a living."

It was the one and only time I ever laughed about MeToo,
but …

I couldn't control myself, and it felt kind of good.

5/17/2021

The Hourglass

On this day carved out for mothers, motherhood begets
maternal bonds. Push, push, push the hourglass away.
The sand, the mother, the child, all flowing down, down,
down. And the sand is boulder-heavy, from brunches that never
happen to nonexistent flowers and sentimental cards that are
never sent and never received. Like an hourglass, I measure
the intervals of time.
Time left,
the end of time,
the passage of time.
Two fragile bulbs of glass
and
free-flowing sand. A reminder
of the thing to come. This time shall pass.
Time heals all wounds, you'll see. But I don't see the healing, just
the passing. And then a phone call from the littlest ones singing "Happy
Birthday," even though it's Mother's Day. There is nothing, nothing,
nothing, that compares. As they sing, the hourglass fades and melts away.

5/8/2022

The Words I Never Said

My heart breaks for you because I know too well
the devastation of it.

I told you that MeToo consumes me and feeds on everything good
and decent in my life.

You opened up and told me the unthinkable, and then,
through blinding tears,
you asked me if any of it could ever be forgotten.

I hugged you tightly, but I never answered.
So now I will.

I've tried to push it away, get over it, move on, and shut up
to appease the others.

But no, I will never forget my fourteen-year-old self.
I see her in every mirror, every photo, and every crooked smile.

I want to see her tenacity, her courage, her kindness.
But all I ever see is her helpless heap of flesh and bones.

6/6/2022

The Unraveling

How do I put into words my high school reunion #51 without being overly telling or excessively revealing?

A poem, yes, a poem is illusory and concealing, concealing like gray hair, hidden under highlights and lowlights, and skin lotions and miracle potions slathered on wrinkled, sagging skin.

There were the dearest of old friends and a spattering of new, and others I no longer imagine sharing a park bench with—like the bookends we once were. Yes, Paul, ♪ how terribly strange to be seventy ♪.

Missed chances at possible true love and what-if sliding doors. A drive-by of this house and that house, and this school and that school, and waiting in a parking lot for church bells that never rang.

Some clicks pleasantly surprised me, while other cliques were still in social play, a reminder that some things never change.

And then came a devastating and unapologetic confession, fifty-four years too late, about a jock-joining sexually deviant quartet I had no memory of.

His detailed words still make my skin crawl. "We passed you around, but you fought like hell and gave one of us a bloody nose, so we let you go."

And just like that, all the progress I fought to achieve unraveled in a never-ending ball, like the ripping and removing of the ruinous stitches in a knitting project that otherwise would be too noticeable to ignore.

10/4/2022

A Work in Progress

I'm not perfect.

I never have been.

I never will be.

I'm still that scrappy girl

trying to figure stuff out.

I'm a work in progress, and

I'm okay with that.

7/21/2023

I See You

I see you in the majesty of the star-dotted stratosphere.
And when the clouds darken the ominous skies, I see you.

Among the trees or the whispering wind or the last
fluttering of the butterflies, I see you.

When a young child flies by me on a bicycle
or chases after an errant ball, I see you.

I once saw you on a train, causing my broken heart to
spasm and spill out all over me.

I saw you just yesterday in the Judean desert
and at the bar, downing a cocktail.

And when that bucking ibex locked eyes with
me, yes, oh yes, it was you that I saw.

Every so often, I see you in the ocean.

Sometimes, the ocean is me—calm and tranquil until I see you—
and then I am a rip current, plunging under, way, way out of reach.

I packed up the photos, stored the first place trophies,
and stashed away all that would remind me.

But still, I see you.

8/30/2023

One Holiday at a Time

Today, the day before
another holiday,
I picked this up
and that up and
felt powerless things.

Thirteen are coming,
but one will be missing.

I brace myself for another
holiday without fourteen.

Fourteen is the dream.

But not today.

Today, I'm preparing myself for
thirteen.

Today, I feel like Dorothy's
rusted Tin Man, but in reverse.

I don't want a heart.

11/23/2023

Lifeline

I needed to know if he knew.

The others I told dismissed the
devastation the high school
reunion confession instilled in me.

I felt emotionally misunderstood.

Invalidated. Alone.

But I don't harbor any ill feelings.

Every relationship has its landscape,

its limits.

I took a chance and phoned a friend.

And, oh, he proved his worth.

He was going to do his best
to help make me whole.

He was going to take
matters into his own hands.

He was my lifeline.

But then he died.

12/17/2023

The End

The finale of this poetic timeline is coming to an end.
But nowhere near the end end.
So, the timeline continues.
I had a plan, but the plan had other plans,
like the obituary that never came to pass.
I am sickened by the thought that he will outlive me.
How twisted a fate that would be.
But then again, I'll be dead.
That's how this nightmare might all end.

1/1/2024

ME TOO: A POETIC TIMELINE

Somewhere Under the Rainbow

Him: "You haven't been yourself these past few days. Are you okay?"

Her: "Aw, that's so sweet, but don't worry about me. I'm fine."

Him: "No, you're not. I can tell. What's wrong?"

Her: "You're just a kid. You don't need to hear my tales of woe."

Him: "I want to hear about what makes you so sad. It helps me to know that there's someone else out there who's struggling, like me."

Her: "We all struggle. It's the people you would never guess who sometimes struggle the most. I'm so sorry you struggle, too. You know you can tell me anything."

Him: "Then you tell me, and next time, I'll tell you."

Her: "I don't know. You're too young to hear about certain stuff."

Him: "No, I'm not too young. I've been through a lot of things."

Her: "That makes me very upset. I wish I could make those things go away."

Him: "If you don't tell me what's wrong, I'll be upset that you don't trust me with your things."

Her: "It's not something many want to hear. And it might make you anxious."

Him: "I'm always anxious. I want to understand you. Maybe I can help you."

Her: "Okay, but only because your love gives me courage, and you're among the few people I trust. I was sexually abused as a child."

Him: "Oh no. Can I give you a hug?"

Her: "Yes, please."

Him: "Hugs always help."

Her: "Yes, they do. Especially hugs from you. But please, don't tell anyone what I just told you."

Him: "I would never say one word. You should know that about me."

Her: "I do know that about you."

Him: "Was this person someone you knew?"

Her: "Yes."

Him: "I'm sorry you're crying. But I'm glad you told me. Was this person someone you loved?"

Her: "Yes."

Him: "Can you tell me who it was?"

Her: "Oh, no. I couldn't do that."

Him: "Can you give me a hint?"

Her: "It was a family member."

Him: "That's really awful."

Her: "Yeah, awful indeed. That's why I try to be especially kind and gentle to those I love."

Him: "You're kind and gentle because that's who you are."

Her: "Maybe. But please, this conversation stays between us, right?"

Him: "Your secret is safe with me. But people should know."

5/27/2024

Me Too: A Poetic Timeline

The End End

Instead of amen, I catechize for a sign, any old sign.
Constantly searching for a spiritually charged lifeline.

Something, anything to allay my fears.
A ghostly way to wipe away my tears.

For most of my life, I've regularly summoned my deceased.
Because if and when they appear, all of my darkness gets released.

To quell the mental din, I implore them to please stop by.
Only then do I feel protected against the wrath of his ever-evil eye.

But his death—the end that I patiently waited for, totally surprised me.
I didn't feel vindicated, I didn't feel safe, and I definitely didn't feel free.

I wasn't sad, but I wasn't glad; shockingly, there was no relief.
And his demise did nothing to assuage my lifelong, immutable grief.

Please, oh please, I kept saying aloud, I don't want any signs from you.
You did enough damage to me when you were alive; hashtag Me Too.

Let's leave it all unsaid; a sign from you I don't want or need.
While you rest in peace, I'm still trying to quell my slow bleed.

6/16/2024

ABOUT THE AUTHOR

Teri Schure is the founder of the international news website Worldpress.org, a freelance journalist, writer, blogger, and business consultant.

Her blog, The Teri Tome, attracts over 30,000 page views per month, plus an additional 50,000 on Worldpress.org.

Teri has been an executive director at Newsweek, a publisher and COO of World Press Review magazine, and in 2007, was Commentary magazine's first female publisher since its founding in 1945.

Her first novel, *Our Romantic Getaway*, was published in 2014; a children's book, *The Day It Snowed Popcorn*, in 2019; and *Tarot For Beginners*, in 2024.

For more information about Teri, her life's storms, frailties, shortcomings, and random musings, go to her blog at blog.terischure.com or her author website at terischure.com.

www.ingramcontent.com/pod-product-compliance
Lightning Source LLC
Chambersburg PA
CBHW082212070526
44585CB00020B/2377